Useful Tips for your Health and your Portfolio

By Loren Collar

Loren Collar holds a PhD in financial economics and has worked at different banks and financial services.

Verlag: BoD · Books on Demand GmbH, Überseering 33,
22297 Hamburg, bod@bod.de
Druck: Libri Plureos GmbH, Friedensallee 273, 22763 Hamburg
ISBN: 978-3-6963-7798-4

FSC www.fsc.org
MIX
Papier aus verantwortungsvollen Quellen
Paper from responsible sources
FSC® C105338

Content

This book is an expression of opinion and not financial advice. The funds presented here are examples and should not be taken as individual recommendations. Please note that investments can involve risks.

The validity of the content is limited to the day of publication.

Prolog

Everyone in the forties wants to be healthy and wants to live forever. You also overthink your financial situation whether you have to work forever or whether your money is sufficient for your retirement. You just have to overthink your situation whether your body is strong enough and your salary is huge enough for your financial independence. Here are the best tips for your health and for your portfolio for the near future.

Analyse your own body

First of all you should have a look at your own body. Perhaps you feel there is something you could do for your health. You think you could or should loose weight or do some easy workouts. But you don't know how to start or whether there is something to do in your forties.

Perhaps you work at an office and you have to sit from nine to five and just eat some snacks because there is not enough time for lunch break.

You will probably recognize that this is not very good for your health till the end of your forties.

So what is to do?

Have you thought about analyzing your lifestyle and your own body?

There is the so called body mass index which shows your health regarding your weight and your length.

BMI= weight (kg)/ length (m^2).

- < 18,5: Underweight
- 18,5 - 24,9: Normal weight
- 25,0 - 29,9: Overweight
- >30,0: Obesity

In case you are underweight you should check your health at your doctor.

In case you are overweight you should work on healthy food and your fitness including workouts. In the following there are some nice easy workouts you can do every morning. There will be also some good tips for some easy healthy little food snacks you could prepare in the evening before your next day at work. You should always do some meal preps because it is much more healthier than fast food.

What are your aims to loose weight?

- **Perhaps you eat at work some snacks the whole day and than get hungry at home. So you put a large pizza in the oven and after that you eat some chocolate bars. Then you wonder why you gain weight?**

But what is the right thing to do?

„You should meal prep every evening with healthy food to avoid eating snacks at work"

In case you don't like salad there are also some nice healthy alternative you could prepare. So never leave the house without some self-made food-snacks.

So as said it depends on your own situation right now. Your homework for today is to analyze your own body and look into the future: what do you want to achieve?

Perhaps you also plan to loose weight while still working or you want to get a stronger body.So it also depends on your health and your lifestyle.

Analyse your financial situation

Next you should analyze your own risk situation in your life and of your portfolio.
What did you achieve in your mid life and what are your aims?

- **Perhaps you live in your forties with your wife and you like your jobs. You own a small house in a suburb and you have a small banking account.**

„Perhaps you should buy some investment funds"

It depends on your own situation that you have to analyze for yourself now. In case you have to pay the mortgages rates of your own house or your consumer loans it would be another. Perhaps you have more debt to pay off, so that you just have to calculate when is the time to be out of debt. Don't follow the advice to get into debt again and invest at the same time. So you couldn't get out of the debt situation to become a large investor.

So as said it depends on your own situation right now. You have to analyze your own balance sheet and to look into the future: what do you want to achieve? In case you want to keep your luxury lifestyle on traveling, new cars and expensive restaurants, you probably need more money for the future. So you have to work quite longer in your fifties before you reach the retirement age.

Perhaps you also plan to work during your retirement as a gardener or as a nanny. So it also depends on your health and your lifestyle. Additionally you have to consider the inflation rate and also care costs.

You also have to consider the gap between your salary now and your pension. In order to close that gap you have to consider a perfect return of your investments.

Investment in ETFs

The investment in one ETF MSCI world could be one part of the strategy.

But be aware that all those MSCI World ETFs are highly correlated to each other and that you have to mix them with some other global funds.

The disadvantages of MSCI World ETFs are their large US shares, a lot of tech stocks and they contain no emerging markets.

So have a look at some great funds which have a large replicated index like an ETF. Such funds replicate an index like the NASDEQ or the DAX so that you have all those single titles diversified in your portfolio. In addition such an ETF is free of charge and ongoing fees are much more cheaper. Perhaps you choose the MSCI world fund which has a great diversification or just buy three or four ETFs that replicate the share markets of US, Europe, Japan or emerging markets.

Unlike the well-known MSCI World, such indices, which include the MSCI All Country World (ACWI) and the FTSE All World, are broader in scope. They contain significantly more companies than the MSCI World and invest in both developed and emerging markets. The MSCI World, which ranks third with inflows of over one billion euros, only includes companies from developed countries.

So don't invest just in one ETF, even not only in the MSCI world, because there is also a country cluster in the US in those funds.

In order to avoid such country agglomeration you should invest in different ETFs: global (perhaps Europe) and also the world wide index MSCI.

Plan a buffer

The safety buffer could help you in case market prices decline.

„You should plan a buffer"

In case you buy a share or a fund there is always the risk of paying too much.

You should plan a safety margin so called buffer in case you assign the fund with a value of $200 and it is only worth $190. So your buffer is $10.

So that you've already calculated the loss within the buffer.

Otherwise the fund could be worth $210 so that your profit is $10 and with the calculation of a buffer.

But it isn't that easy to determine the buffer that is the difference between the actual value and the purchasing price.

The price of a share is determined on the stock exchange, but the real value is an other thing.

The past cash flows of a company is the key figure for valuation.
Here the buffer is the difference between the expected value and the share price. So you predict the value of the last year's profit and assume the same growth of the last year.

If you are more conservative you plan also some other circumstances and add 10 percent to a lower growth. So your buffer will be larger cause of some special surroundings.
You should also be aware whether you are more risk oriented or more conservative. That depends on the calculation of your buffer, but it is also a tendency whether you resist to some market turbulence with your buffer.

How large this buffer should be depends also on your situations of life whether you are just a beginner at work or a retiree who lives off his returns on investment. And also don’t forget that money on a bank account loses it’s value due to inflation.

Investment in gold

Gold can indeed protect against inflation and geopolitical risks, but it's also not a reliable protection in every situation.

You mix a small amount of gold reserve to your portfolio. But be careful of the fees and costs of banks when you put it into their safes. You could leave a small amount of the asset in your own safes at home, but be careful that you have an insurance at home. Also in insecure times like wars or even customs explode, gold is a secure haven.

„Gold is a secure haven"

Also have a look at the index „Nyse Arca Gold Bugs" (HUI) which actually has a great 1-year performance, but a high 1-year volatility.

Despite the sector would be a great investment for your single stocks which you could mix to your portfolio in small percentage.

And now let's have a look at the asset silver. Silver is a great asset because it is cheaper than gold when you buy it. But it has great chances to grow up as markets raise in products like photovoltaic, electronic mobility or semiconductors. On the other hand there's the risk that the prices of silver could change due to changes of economic situations. There is a great demand of silver in the solar industry's production, so that the silver prices could change due to changes in that production.

Maybe a combination of both underlyings - silver and gold - in your ETF portfolio is a great opportunity.
Even if gold disappoints in recent weeks, it can provide stability in uncertain times.

Diversification

Crucial is a broadly diversified portfolio across sectors, regions, and company sizes, including both developed and emerging markets, large corporations, small and medium-sized enterprises (SMEs).

Strategically oriented ETFs, such as value or quality strategies, can be a useful addition, because even by falling markets, individual segments perform differently.
Modern Portfolio Theory (MPT)[1] is a well known mathematical approach to portfolio selection by considering the relation of risk and return. See behind the key principles of Modern Portfolio Theory of Harry M. Markowitz:

* First it is important to diversify investments across different asset classes (stocks, bonds and others). You should choose investments across different assets with different risks and returns. By combining some assets that have not a correlation equal 1 (not perfectly correlated) this model provides you a more efficient risk-return trade-off.

* Then the efficient frontier gives the portfolios with the highest expected return for a given level of risk or the lowest risk for a given level of expected return.

---

[1] See Harry M. Markowitz: *Portfolio Selection*. In: Journal of Finance, 7, 1952

You receive the efficient frontier by combining assets in different proportions, considering their expected returns, volatilities, and correlations.
Now you see the requirement for greater expected risks for greater expected returns: The ideal portfolio for the market is obtained when a portfolio exists on the Capital Market Line (CML)[2].

By choosing an appropriate ETF, perhaps a MSCI world fund you diversify your portfolio with all over the world titles
Diversification is good to mitigate losses, but be aware that there might also be some.
Besides the MSCI world fund has the greatest liquidity.

On the other hand you should contribute a few other mixed funds for your „personal single risk".
Those mixed funds could be an alternative to the world indices. But notice that they are much more expensive than ETFs. But they could be a little bit less riskier. So a mixture of both alternative products as said before will be a good diversification for your portfolio.

The advantage of property funds is that they invest in different properties or classes of properties so that the risk is much higher diversified. You can also benefit from higher rents in different locations of the properties which are almost in profitable cities.
So also rents and location of the properties are a important part of the investment strategy.

---

2 See William F. Sharpe: Capital asset prices: A theory of market equilibrium under conditions of risk, In: Journal of Finance, 19, 1964

Investment in properties

You can invest in properties, in different regions and cities. Perhaps you have to renovate it in some cases.

„The location is the core factor of properties"

You have to choose the right location of a property.

Additionally you have to pay the notary, the brokerage fees and also the land register entry.

Besides you probably need a mortgage in order to finance the house price. But the repayment rate should not exceed 35% of your net monthly income. If it exceeds this limit, you should look for a more affordable house or flat. In addition you should decide between predictable fixed rates and variable rates.

After that you can start your property search. The location should be chosen next to services and infrastructure like subway station and supermarkets..

You should choose a flat you will like and which is nice for you in a big city.

So you have a lot to do with the search for a good property and than have to negotiate with the pre-owners. Perhaps you need a credit from your bank and don't forget the notary costs.

Also have a look at the previous payment of the pre-owner in the files if there is something strange in the documents.

You could have a look at the location of the house or flat at other times of the day in order to get an impression of its environment.

The location is the most important thing of the selection because it is much easier to rent a good located flat to someone than one in the suburbs.

Also don't exceed your budget-limit because in addition you have to pay taxes for the property and the land registry enter is also expensive depending on the country you are living in.

Besides the constitution of the flat or house should be good or it should be easy for you to renovate it. So it depends on your own constitution because if you are able to renovate it yourself, you could buy an old cheap property and then renovate it. But if you have to pay the renovation costs and some electricians and plumbers it will be cleverer to buy a new one.

Perhaps you find a good location in New York:

DON'T BLOCK
THE BOX
FINE + 2 POINTS
HOTEL
NEW YORKER
SYSCO

Investment in healthy food

You should eat the whole day some healthy snacks and in the evening you could cook a great meal of Mediterranean food. This includes tomatoes, aubergines, zucchini and onions.

Don't eat too fast and invest in organic products you could get at a nearby market.

You can cultivate your own organic fruits. This is very easy with tomatoes or zucchini. Just put some seeds in March or April in a box filled with peat and give it some water every day. Then in summer you could pick some nice tomatoes.

At the weekend you should meal-prep some nice **beef stews**. These are very easy to make in a pressure cooker. Just put some beef with salt, pepper, juniper berries, a little bit of nutmeg, some carrots and a liter of water in a pressure cooker for one hour.

You could put some cooked noodles or rice in it and then prep it in the refrigerator for the next week.

There is also an easy recipe to get your own nice bread like a **ciabatta**:

400g flour
1 little spoon salt
1 little spoon natron
1 great spoon olive oil

1 hour in the oven at 180 degrees in the middle at recirculating air.

You can eat this in the evening with some avocados, tomatoes and cheese.

There is also an easy recipe for some nice **beef roulades**:
Recipe 3 beef roulades:
3 beef filets
Mustard
Pepper and salt
Pickels
Bacon

Put some mustard on the beef filet and salt and pepper over it. Then one pickle and a piece of bacon in it and roll it around, fix it with some tooth picks. Then put it in the oven with some carrots, onions and some beef sauce about 190 degrees for one hour.

Investment in Technologies

There is always a great market in technology shares. The title Micron Technology (ISIN US5951121038) is one of the semiconductor manufacturers who could have great potential to perform in the next future.

Also Fair Isaac and Axon Enterprises (US05464C1018) could be on growth again.
Besides SMA Solar Technology, Siltronic AG, Alzchem Group have great potential.

And surely Nvidia is a great title to invest in.

The best US titles are the well known Apple (US0378331005), Microsoft, Amazon (US0231351067), Tesla, Meta and Alphabet with great growth.

The Nasdaq 100 is the important US-technology index you could invest in, so you just should look on its titles and take one of its biggest. But be aware that these titles mentioned above are only some examples of good investments in technology, there are always some others you could choose on Bloomberg or Reuters.

The largest part of your portfolio should be diversified in shares all over the world. You could invest in the ETF MSCI world like the MSCI All Countries World Index or the FTSE All World index. So that could be part of your strategy to invest in shares all over the world, not in one single title. The second part of your portfolio should be hold in global ETFs of your home country (maybe in Europe or USA). So don't invest just in one ETF, even not only in the MSCI world, because there is also a country cluster in the US in those funds. In order to avoid such country agglomeration you should invest in different ETFs: global (perhaps Europe) and also the world wide index MSCI. For the remaining part of your portfolio you can choose some single titles of bonds or shares that you personally like.

Or some ETF of the FTSE Developed World (see all titles on finance.net):
Like Vanguard FTSE Developed World ETF Distributing (IE00BKX55T58)
Volatility (1Y): 10%
Sharpe ratio (1Y): +1.39
Its countries:
66% US
7% Japan
3% UK
3% Canada
Biggest positions (see on finance.net)

Name	ISIN	Weight
NVIDIA Corp	US67066G1040	4.71 %
Apple Inc	US0378331005	4.38 %
Microsoft Corp	US5949181045	3.31 %
Amazon.com Inc	US0231351067	2.29 %
Alphabet Inc Class A	US02079K3059	2.06 %
Broadcom Inc	US11135F1012	1.68 %
Alphabet Inc Class C	US02079K1079	1.67 %
Meta Platforms Inc Class A	US30303M1027	1.61 %

Or the Franklin FTSE Developed World ETF (IE000CVOSY02):

Volatility (1Y): 10%
Sharpe ratio (1Y): +1.38
Its countries:
67% US
6% Japan
3% UK
3% Canada
Biggest positions (see on finance.net):

Name	ISIN	Weight
NVIDIA Corp	US67066G1040	5.25 %
Apple Inc	US0378331005	4.33 %
Microsoft Corp	US5949181045	3.44 %
Amazon.com Inc	US0231351067	2.69 %
Alphabet Inc Class A	US02079K3059	2.21 %
Broadcom Inc	US11135F1012	2.07 %
Alphabet Inc Class C	US02079K1079	1.79 %
Meta Platforms Inc Class A	US30303M1027	1.65 %

Tesla Inc	US88160R1014	1.25 %
Berkshire Hathaway Inc Class B	US0846707026	0.98 %

Or the Vanguard FTSE Developed World UCITS ETF USD Accumulation (IE00BK5BQV03):
Volatility (1Y): 11%
Sharpe ratio (1Y): +1.39
Its countries:
66% US
7% Japan
3% UK
3% Canada
Biggest positions (see on finance.net):

Name	ISIN	Weight
NVIDIA Corp	US67066G1040	4.71 %
Apple Inc	US0378331005	4.38 %
Microsoft Corp	US5949181045	3.31 %
Amazon.com Inc	US0231351067	2.29 %
Alphabet Inc Class A	US02079K3059	2.06 %
Broadcom Inc	US11135F1012	1.68 %
Alphabet Inc Class C	US02079K1079	1.67 %
Meta Platforms Inc Class A	US30303M1027	1.61 %

Tesla Inc	US88160R1014	1.29 %
Eli Lilly and Co	US5324571083	0.96%

Or the Vanguard FTSE All-World ETF (IE00B3RBWM25):
Volatility (1Y): 11%
Sharpe ratio (1Y): +1.34
Its countries:
60% US
6% Japan
3% UK
3% China
Biggest positions (see on finance.net):

Name	ISIN	Weight
NVIDIA Corp	US67066G1040	4.22 %
Apple Inc	US0378331005	3.92 %
Microsoft Corp	US5949181045	2.96 %
Amazon.com Inc	US0231351067	2.05 %
Alphabet Inc Class A	US02079K3059	1.85 %
Taiwan Semiconductor Manufacturing Co Ltd	TW0002330008	1.58 %
Broadcom Inc	US11135F1012	1.5 %
Alphabet Inc Class C	US02079K1079	1.5 %

Meta Platforms Inc Class A	US30303M1027	1.44 %
Tesla Inc	US88160R1014	1.16%

As you can see these titles all depend on the markets in US or Europe or Japan. In case there is a world crash all those titles will decline. So be careful and don't put all your money in these ETFs. You could also invest in the next ETF which is more European and you should mix them with other investments.

Or iShares Core FTSE 100 ETF (IE0005042456):
Volatility (1Y): 11%
Sharpe ratio (1Y): +1.49
Its countries:
92% UK
3% Switzerland
1% Hong Kong
Biggest positions(see on finance.net):

Name	ISIN	Weight
HSBC Holdings PLC	GB0005405286	8.98 %
AstraZeneca PLC	GB0009895292	8.7 %
Shell PLC	GB00BP6MXD84	7.47 %
Rolls-Royce Holdings PLC	GB00B63H8491	4.33 %
Unilever PLC	GB00BVZK7T90	3.54 %
British American Tobacco PLC	GB0002875804	3.46 %
BP PLC	GB0007980591	3.45 %
GSK PLC	GB00BN7SWP63	3.4 %

Rio Tinto PLC Ordinary Shares	GB0007188757	2.94 %
BAE Systems PLC	GB0002634946	2.61 %

Or Invesco FTSE All-World UCITS ETF Acc (IE000716YHJ7)
Volatility (1Y): 11%
Sharpe ratio (1Y): +1.35
Its countries:
61% US
6% Japan
3% UK
3% Canada
3% China
Biggest positions(see on finance.net):

Name	ISIN	Weight
NVIDIA Corp	US67066G1040	4.56 %
Apple Inc	US0378331005	3.83 %
Microsoft Corp	US5949181045	2.94 %
Amazon.com Inc	US0231351067	2.36 %
Alphabet Inc Class A	US02079K3059	1.92 %
Broadcom Inc	US11135F1012	1.81 %
Taiwan Semiconductor Manufacturing Co Ltd	TW0002330008	1.58 %
Alphabet Inc Class C	US02079K1079	1.55 %

Meta Platforms Inc Class A	US30303M1027	1.43 %
Tesla Inc	US88160R1014	1.02 %

Be aware that there are a lot of other good ETFs you can find on finance.net or Bloomberg. These mentioned above are only examples and are not an advice to buy. It's just for your information that there are good ETFs to diversify your portfolio and to get secure to some market turbulences. Just inform yourself on the common webpages like Bloomberg or Reuters.

PENNSYLVANIA

Investment in your fitness

Go to your opened window and do some simple stretches every morning. It is really important for your mind and your whole body to relax. You have to round your arms about 10 times first left around and than otherwise.
Second just walk five minutes on the same place and breathe at the open window. Then you could relax and get your mind in a new fresh way, you will see decisions will be made very easy after that little work out. It's just the mixture of fresh air and your relaxation of the body.

„ The workout routine every morning is very important for your mind"

After that you could make a healthy green tea and eat some nice oats with some fresh fruits.

But be aware that also a quick walk in the lunch break is very effective to your health. Just get out of the office in the fresh air in order to cool your mind and get some new ideas for your project. That is really very effective for your brain and your health.

Besides your intelligence is better and your body is much more fitter.

In the evening you could do some cycling or walking just what you like to be prepared for the next day and to slow down your mind and your thoughts of the whole day at work.

Investment in Digitals

There is also a great new market in crypto.
It is dominated by Bitcoin (BTC), Ethereum (ETH) or the crypto currency XRP.
But be aware that these markets are really speculative and a total loss is always possible. Because there is no regulation on these markets. Even your house bank does not sell every product of these categories. So be careful with those investments.

„ Perhaps put a small amount of your money in crypto“

Use a small percentage of your salary to those „gambling techniques“ in order to get a feeling of those products. But don't put too much in those not regulated products.

Don't look after the amount of money you've invested long-term too often while using a trading app.

In addition with a savings plan you can invest small amounts and use the independence of the current fund price or share price.

Besides as your living conditions change you have to adjust your portfolio to your new lifestyle.

Perhaps you like to invest in something new in order to learn how it works and whether it is profitable. But just a small percentage of your liquidity should be taken. Don't touch your money you have to invest for your daily demands.

Learn patience

Be patient and don't get too nervous as the markets move downwards. Also be patient in case you don't loose weight that easily you have planed.

„Don't be too nervous in case there is a crisis."

Things will get better in a few months. Don't react to quick to some market turbulences. There are always ups and downs in the markets like the Lehman crash or the real estate crash in the US and those derivatives. You don't need all the money in the funds or your depot. Just let time pass away and have a look in the next few months.

It's the same to your body weight and your health. Sometimes it is easy to loose weight and sometimes you don't success and you gain again. But don't get frustrated on your body because there are also ups and downs like on the markets. It's always like a sinus curve which goes up and similar goes down. But as you know after that there is always an up-time again.

Be aware that your portfolio should always be a mixture of different products like ETFs in different countries as well as different industries. So it doesn't depend on market turbulences in any industry or country.

Appendix

Examples of neo brokers with robot advisors:

Scalable Capital
No depot fees

Evergreen
Evergreen comfort evergreen balance evergreen growth Strategies

eToro
No depot fees

N26
ETFs on MSCI World, MSCI Emerging Markets or S&P500.

Smartbroker+
No depot fees but order costs

Bunq
Trade fees and order costs

willBe Invest
Robot advisor in Lichtenstein but has depot fees

Quirion
Savings plan as a product

Robot advisor of Quirin private bank but has depot fees

Bevestor
Depot fees
Savings plan

LIQID
Depot fees
No savings plan

Fidelity
Depot fees
Savings plan

Smavesto
Depot fees and other fees
Savings plan

Examples of useful links:

bloomberg.com

reuters.com

onvista.com

nasdaq.com

Examples of useful books:

* An Introduction to Mutual Funds Worldwide by Ray Russell

* Abnormal Returns by Tadas Viskanta

* Black-Scholes and Beyond by Chriss, Neil A.

* Backstage Wall Street: An Insider's Guide to Knowing Who to Trust, Who to Run from, and How to Maximize Your Investments by Joshua M. Brown

* Encyclopedia of Alternative Investments by Greg N. Gregoriou

* Exchange-Traded Funds For Dummies by Russell Wild

* ETF Investment Strategies: Best Practices from Leading Experts on Constructing a Winning ETF Portfolio by Aniket Ullal

* ETF Fundamentals - Core Concepts and Market Mechanics (The ETF Edge Vol.1) by Marco Colombo

* Financial Statement Analysis by Martin S. Fridson; Fernando Alvarez

* Foreign Exchange
Practical Asset Pricing and Macroeconomic Theory
by Adam S. Iqbal

* Frequently Asked Questions in Quantitative Finance: Including Key Models, Important Formulae, Common Contracts, a History of Quantitative Finance, Sundry Lists, Brainteasers and More by Paul Wilmott.

* Guide to Financial Markets by Marc Levinson

* Guide to Investment Strategy: How to Understand Markets, Risk, Rewards and Behaviour by Peter Stanyer

* How the Trading Floor Really Works by Duhon Duhon; Terri Dun

* How to Read a Financial Report: Wringing Vital Signs Out of the Numbers by John A. Tracy

* Investors and Markets: Portfolio Choices, Asset Prices, and Investment Advice by William F. Sharpe

* Inside the Black Box: The Simple Truth About Quantitative Trading by Rishi K. Nearing

* Investment Banking Explained: An Insider's Guide to the Industry by Michel Fleuriet

* Investment Mistakes: Even Smart Investors Make and How to Avoid Them by Larry E. Swedroe; R. C. Balaban
* Long-Term Secrets to Short-Term Trading by Larry Williams

* Manias, Panics, and Crashes: A History of Financial Crises by Robert Z. Aliber; Charles P. Kindleberger

* Market Sense and Nonsense: How the Markets Really Work (and how they don't) by Jack D. Schwager; Joel Greenblatt

* More Money Than God: Hedge Funds and the Making of a New Elite by Sebastian Mallaby

* Narrative and Numbers: The Value of Stories in Business by Aswath Damodaran

* Other People's Money: Inside the Housing Crisis and the Demise of the Greatest Real Estate Deal Ever Made by Charles V. Bagli

* Option Volatility Trading Strategies (Wiley Trading) by Sheldon Natenberg

* Pioneering Portfolio Management: An Unconventional Approach to Institutional Investment by David F. Swensen.

* Pricing the Future: Finance, Physics, and the 300-Year Journey to the Black-Scholes Equation: A Story of Genius and Discovery by George G. Szpiro

* Private Equity at Work: When Wall Street Manages Main Street by Eileen Applebaum; Rosemary Batt

* Stalking the Black Swan: Research and Decision-Making in a World of Extreme Volatility by Kenneth A. Posner

* The Essays of Warren Buffett: Lessons for Corporate America by Warren E. Buffett; Lawrence A. Cunningham

* The ETF Book: All You Need to Know About Exchange-Traded Funds, Updated Edition
by R. A. Ferri

* The Financial Numbers Game: Detecting Creative Accounting Practices by Charles W. Mulford and Eugene E. Comiskey

* The Handbook of Commercial Real Estate Investing by John McMahan

* The Investor's Dilemma: How Mutual Funds are Betraying Your Trust and What to Do About It by Louis Lowenstein

* The Little Book of Common Sense Investing by John C. Bogle

* The Little Book of Market Wizards Lessons from the greatest Traders by Jack D. Schwager

*The Wall Street Primer: The Players, Deals, and Mechanics of the U.S. Securities Market by Jason A. Pedersen

* The Incredible Shrinking Alpha: And What You Can Do to Escape Its Clutches by Larry E. Swedroe; Andrew L. Berkin

* The Intelligent Investor by Benjamin Graham and Jason Zweig

* The Investment Answer: Learn to Manage Your Money and Protect Your Financial Future by Daniel C. Goldie And Gordon S. Murray

* The Wisdom of Finance: Discovering Humanity in the World of Risk and Return by Mihir Desai

* The Mutual Fund Business by Robert C. Pozen and Sandra D. Crane

* The Myth of the Rational Market: Wall Street's Impossible Quest for Predictable Markets by Justin Fox

* The Physics of Wall Street: A Brief History of Predicting the Unpredictable by James Owen Weatherall

* Understanding Wall Street by Jeffrey B. Little

* Visual Guide to Financial Markets by David Wilson

* Volatility Practical Options Theory by Adam S. Iqbal

* Volatility Trading (Wiley Trading Series) by Euan Sinclair

* Wall Street Potholes: Insights from Top Money Managers on Avoiding Dangerous Products by Simon A. Lack

* Wall Streeters: The Creators and Corrupters of American Finance by Edward L. Morris
* What Happened to Goldman Sachs: An Insider's Story of Organizational Drift and its Unintended Consequences by Steven Mandis; Steven G. Mandis

* What Investors Really Want: Discover What Drives Investor Behavior and Make Smarter Financial Decisions by Meir Statman